THE TRIALS AND TRIBULATIONS OF A HUSTLER
A Novel by
Shawnqulas V. Cannon

ISBN: 1523610816
ISBN 13: 9781523610815

CONTENTS

Preface

Is life too short, or do we not utilize the precious time we have available to us? Everything in life happens for a reason. The reason I wrote this fictional book, is to give the people something to reflect on. Older people think they know everything, and young people are brainwashed by music. Few people take the time to find their purposes in life. "The purpose of life is to live a life of purpose."

I heard a saying: "If you want to hide something from someone, put the information into a book." *The Trials and Tribulations of a Hustler* touches all aspects of life. I honestly believe each character is very believable and plays a specific role in everybody's life. This book is a deft, morality, coming-of-age tale.

Good karma is a term that we rarely use. If we do good things, good things will happen to us. It's a must that we learn to feed ourselves positive energy.

I want to thank everyone in advance for reading this story. I would like for this book to touch as many hands possible.

I'm really blessed to have had the help of Ms. Coleman and Rickeya Cannon, they really put together the pieces to the puzzle. Without their hard work, dedication, and continuous prayer *The Trials and Tribulations of a Hustler* wouldn't be here.

#SocialShawn

Chapter One: A Mother's Struggle

Life is not an option; it is a choice. Growing up in

Memphis, Tennessee, brings automatic doubt and struggle

into our lives. Coming from an unfortunate family or no

family at all, or alternatively, having no mentor or

counselor in our lives, we could be jarred very quickly.

Trouble is easy to get into but hard to get out of. For some

of us, it takes getting caught or jammed up to actually learn

needful lessons. This is very backward to me, knowing

right from wrong. To whom it may concern, as young

people we have to understand that every decision we make

has a consequence. We have to determine whether those

consequences are positive or negative. If we strive and keep

God as our guide, things will get better later.

My name is Chris V. Johnson, and I resided in Memphis, Tennessee. I arrived in this tragic city in October 1995. I was not born in a big, fancy neighborhood where everyone kept their grass cut and greeted one another daily. I was also not born in the "hood," where you could get jumped for just riding your new bike down the street. However, I did come from a family of struggle and prayer. We didn't have too much or too little, but we had just enough to get by.

Ebony Johnson is my mother's name. She gave birth to me at the tender age of fourteen. She was still learning and developing herself. Having a child and balancing school could be very challenging at times, not to mention coming home to a drunk mother every day and a "playa" for a stepdaddy.

My granny would say to her, "You're so dumb, and you don't have any money. How you expect to feed a child?" She never meant any of those hurtful comments. The alcohol just took control, and she had no control of her mouth.

Real Deal Phil, as he was known on the streets, was Granny's boyfriend. He was a Mississippi pimp who was feared by many. He never worked a day in his life, but he kept a bankroll in his pocket. Selling a woman was as easy for him as a basketball layup. He had women selling their bodies all over town, including my mother. What else does a fourteen-year-old single mother do, with no other options to provide for her firstborn?

The father of her first child was Greg Wilson. My father wanted to help, but he had his own problems to deal with. He was eight years older than my mother, with two kids before me. He hustled his whole life, going back and forth, in and out of jail. Parole is a trap for black males.

They put papers on you to encourage you to do the same thing you did before.

Granny hated for him to come around because of his lifestyle. Without an education in Memphis, it becomes survival of the fittest. He had to grind every day to pay the government and take care of his kids. He did that very well for a short period of time. Fast money does not last long in any circumstance.

Greg Wilson was one of the biggest drug dealers in Orange Mound. Dope was his middle name. He had everything you wanted. He had connections all across the city. But one loose domino can kick down the whole wall. *Loyalty* is a strong word in the dope game he played. In the dope game, there were no real friends because everybody wanted what other people had, and they had to get it one way or another—even if that meant killing or snitching on the next runner-up.

Luckily, my dad was blessed to leave the streets and get another chance at life. For fifteen months of supposed glory, he spent fifteen years in prison. In the blink of an eye, he had to adapt to a whole new way of life in prison, not knowing how long his time in the joint would actually be. Too bad life doesn't have a reset button.

Regarding my up and down household, my mother was the second oldest of four misled siblings, who together could be very aggravating. Without my dad around to help take care of me, she had long nights of crying, doubt, and pain running through her veins. Confusion and delusion led her to ask herself many questions: "Are we going to be OK? Will I be able to provide for my child? Will I finish school? God, please guide me in the right direction."

Then, out of nowhere, Real Deal Phil offered her a job that she felt she couldn't refuse, confronting her with the devil's temptation before she could hear from the Word of

God. As Real Deal Phil told her, "Why stress when you can just have sex? Pain and pleasure put together makes green in any kind of weather. Why do something for free when you can sell yourself for more than cheap?"

To her, his words seemed to make sense. She was only fourteen, not yet the legal age to work a job, so having sex seemed like an easy way to get a stack of bills.

Sadly, people will do anything to get money, so you can only imagine what they will do if they lose it. The Word of God gives us needed perspective: "For the love of money is the root of all evil: which while some coveted after, they have erred from the faith, and pierced themselves through with many sorrows" (1 Tim. 6:10, King James Version).

On one cold winter night, my mother was standing on the corner wearing a miniskirt and a bubble coat—with purple fingernail polish, blood-red lipstick, and eyelashes longer than a pencil. She was shaking and pacing back and forth, waiting for a miracle, when a brown Cadillac with bright blue lights pulled up. Behind the wheel was Real Deal Phil, leaning back, high on his schemes. He told her to get in and let her new life begin. They drove and talked while Keith Sweat played in the background.

Finally, they pulled up to the house, and he asked, "How much you got?"

Digging in her coat pocket, she pulled out a grip you couldn't view with a microscope. He skimmed through it, shaking his head with a big smile on his face. Then, as if he'd been bitten by a snake, he jumped out of the car without another word. My mother sat in the car for a while, breathing a sigh of relief and wondering what was next. Eventually, she walked into the house and made her way to her room, safe and sound. Everybody was asleep, including me.

As my mother started to get ready for bed, a creak came from the door as it opened rapidly. As my mother turned her head, Real Deal Phil hit her in the face. He yelled, "You thought I was going to let you slide without my cash?"

"But I had to get my son some Pampers," she replied while holding her face.

"Does it look like I care about any of that?" said Real Deal Phil. Then he forced himself on her, telling her not to scream as tears of fear and confusion streamed down her face.

The next morning was abnormal for my mother. While her siblings all got ready for school, no one noticed her washing the dried tears from her face in the downstairs bathroom. She kissed me and headed out to school with an upside-down smile on.

Having Granny watching me at that time was like raising myself. She could never stay awake, and when she was awake, she often had a cup of liquor in her hands. Real Deal Phil was like a vampire you only saw at night. That kept my granny mad at the world, not having him around. So just imagine anger and morning alcohol breath forced upon you every day.

When two fifteen came, my mother would rush home only to change clothes and makeup for the night, all the while hating this lifestyle more and more every day. You could see the pain in her eyes, but she was determined to keep me from going without.

After a long day of sacrifice and bitterness, she had Real Deal Phil's voice ringing in her head. Telling her mom or anybody with common sense was not an option for her at the moment. My mother's little sisters would not understand because they were too young minded, and she didn't want them to ever experience this kind of struggle. Her brother was too caught up in himself to notice anything.

Then the moment came: she saw my granny sitting at the kitchen table all by herself and wondered if this was the right moment to share what was on her mind. She started walking toward her. But just then an unexpected phone call came through, and Granny answered with no hesitation.

After a while, Granny let out a blood-curdling scream. She had just heard the awful news that Real Deal Phil had been robbed and gunned down on Shelby Drive. As my mother's siblings attempted to console their mother at the loss of her lover, my mother held me in her arms and quietly gave the Lord the utmost praise. After coming to terms with the fact that he could never hurt her again, she realized that once again there was no one to provide for them. Bad as Real Deal Phil was, the family needed a strong male to provide.

After the funeral, Granny had an awakening. She no longer had the urge to drink. Having no man in her life to provide, she saw that her children were her number-one priority. Job interview after job interview she went on to begin a new chapter of being the main provider for her children. Through prayer and unselfish dedication, she was blessed by the Lord to get a position taking care of disabled children. It paid six dollars an hour.

Without Real Deal Phil, things were actually going a lot better for her, but just the same she needed to confess to my mother the reason behind Greg Wilson's incarceration. Granny's confession would devastate my mother. Weeks passed by, Pampers were getting higher, and Granny had had enough. She was not going to hold it in any longer, and she was going to confess.

My mother was actually vomiting in the bathroom when Granny started to reveal to her how Greg had gotten locked up. "Ebony, I'm so sorry," said Granny, "but I take the blame for getting Greg locked up. The police came in while you were at school, looking for Phil's money and drugs. Unfortunately, Greg walked in to drop off Pampers for Chris. I accused him of everything they found in the house." Granny did not know that my mother had a secret of her own. Minutes passed by while Granny explained herself.

Then, raising up off her knees and wiping her mouth while holding her stomach, my mother looked at Granny and said, "Mom, I'm pregnant." Sadly, Granny's jaw dropped, and she began spewing foul names at my mother. Finally, my mother said, "Mom, Phil raped me." Shock and misunderstanding were written all over Granny's face. It was hard for Granny to believe. After all, in her eyes, Real

Deal Phil cared for all of her children too much to have hurt them. However, the look in my mother's eyes helped Granny to realize the truth, that her lover had raped her baby. At that moment of realization, she hugged my mother so tight. They started to cry together like mother and daughter should. They discussed how they would get past this ordeal. They agreed that prayer was the only answer and that better days were ahead.

With time passing day by day, I was only getting older, and my mother had Real Deal Phil's baby. She named her Alexis. Having a baby sister gave me responsibilities at an early age. My mother graduated from high school, working day and night to make sure food was on the table. She refused to make us go through what she had as a child. Even though we were too young to understand truly how she lived, she made sure our lives seemed perfect with or without a father figure. Ebony Johnson made no excuses.

She had her ups and downs, at times wanting to give up on life, period, but walking in faith and not by sight kept her encouraged. She realized that her life was just beginning.

Chapter Two: No Longer a Boy No Yet a Man

Years went by, and I was not getting any younger. We went to school and daycare because my mother's work shifts were crazy. Alexis started walking and talking. She was beginning her first year in school as well.

I was in the third grade at the time, attending Westwood Elementary. I had one of the prettiest teachers in the school. Ms. Black was so fine and always had a smile on her face, but she was very mean to all of us…in the nicest way. We couldn't talk, sleep, or play paper basketball with the trash can, unless we wanted to put our noses in the corner for half the day.

Attention seeking was one of my best hobbies when I was young. Watching Allen Iverson on television every night had me in time-out often. I would always get caught shooting paper balls because the snooty girls would tell on me. I didn't care, because getting in trouble was very cool to me.

One particular day I refused to take a time-out, and Ms. Black told me to call my mother. I almost defecated in my pants in front of the class as they all yelled, "Ooh, you in trouble."

Before I knew it, I said, "So? I don't care," and that made the situation worse. As we walked toward the office, I was scared to death. Once we were in the office, Ms. Black explained to the principal (verbatim) what had transpired. Instead of getting a phone call home, I had a letter labeled "Only to be opened by Mrs. Johnson" stapled to my shirt.

As my lips practically dragged on the concrete, I walked to meet my sister at the four-way stop. She saw that I was upset, so we walked home in silence. My mind was racing, wondering what was in the letter. The closer we got to home, the more nervous I became and the more I bit my fingernails. As we approached the house, Alexis ran to tell my mother about her day. Wishing I had a similar story to tell my mother, I made a dumb decision. Ten seconds later, all I knew was that the letter that was once stapled to my shirt was now in the bottom of my neighbor's trash can.

With a huge smile on my face, I entered the house. My mother didn't hesitate to ask me how my day had been. Swinging around but without making eye contact, I said my day had been awesome. I ran to my room as quickly as possible to avoid any more questions. Before I could close the door, my mother was right behind me. She asked me if I was sure my day was awesome. Though I nodded yes vigorously, I noticed that my mother had a strange smirk on her face as she closed my bedroom door. As she left the house for work, leaving us home alone. I breathed a huge sigh of relief. I slept like a baby that night, knowing that I had dodged a bullet. Little did I know; my problems had just begun.

The next morning, I awoke to five tightly wrapped switches hitting me across my back and lower legs while my mother was screaming, "Don't you ever lie to me again, young man!" I had never been whipped like that before, and tears fell down my face like a river.

A few days later I got a phone call at home for the same exact action with Ms. Black. The more I got spanked, the more immune I got to the effects of it. I started to build a bit of a reputation for myself at school, one that would prove to be hard to break. Everybody wanted to be my friend because I was known as the class clown. That position made me cocky. I gained two best buddies, and there was no turning back. Terrance and Justin were their names. We all lived a block from one another.

The "Migos" is what they called us around the neighborhood. By the age of ten, we were together every day.

We took all the same classes in school. Every weekend the Crystal Palace skating rink was mandatory. From 6:30 p.m. until midnight, that was the place to be on Saturday nights. All the high-school kids and even some of the drop-out dope boys kicked it there. It just so happened that one of those drop-outs was Justin's big brother, "Tank." He got us into the rink free every weekend, making sure nobody messed with us. But we hadn't realized that we were emerging from boyhood to manhood.

My mother always told me, "If you can hang out at the skating rink all night, Sunday morning church service isn't an option; it's a mandate." At that age, church was boring to me without my homies. I actually had to sit down and pay attention. A couple months went by, and I decided something had to change: it was either the Crystal Palace or the Mount Vernon Baptist Church service.

When the next Saturday came around, I told my mother I was going over to Justin's house for the weekend, thinking that we could go to church together. But on my way to Justin's house, a black Monte Carlo pulled up beside me, and Tank and Justin told me to get in. I ignored my feeling of trepidation and hopped in the car that was sitting on twenty-six-inch wheels. We cruised to what looked like a vacant house, and Tank got out, saying, "Wait right here, homies."

He walked across the street with his hoodie pulled over his head, and suddenly there was the *pow*, *pow* sound of gunshots. In the blink of an eye, Tank was back in the car and going in reverse. He was sweating bullets like he had just seen a ghost. Justin was on the passenger side looking confused, and I was in the backseat scared out of my mind.

"Oh, snap!" Tank said as the police and ambulance drove past us. Before Justin or I could ask what was going on, Tank put us out of the car and said he would see us soon. We started walking toward Terrance's house still in a daze, curious as to what happened at that house and wondering if it was all a dream.

As we entered Terrance's driveway, he came running out of the house. "Hey, guys," he yelled. "Somebody is live on the news in a high-speed chase."

Justin and I knew it was Tank. Sure enough, the black Monte Carlo with the twenty-six-inch wheels was on the news. As we watched in horror, Tank's car flipped over several times. As it was reported, the airbag deployed, breaking his neck and killing him instantly. It hurt all of us to see this tragedy happen on television. Tank was well-known all over the city, and he was loved by many. For me to have just been with him less than an hour before he died, really should have been a wake-up call. Instead, it kind of sparked my bad decisions even more.

A week went by, and Tank's funeral was one of the saddest ever. So many rumors surrounded his death. Only Justin and I knew the real story, and that was how we wanted it to stay. It was sad to say, but we never even told Terrance about our car ride on that dreadful day that Tank died. We were just thankful that we hadn't been in that car when it flipped. At least that's how I felt about the situation.

Justin figured he had a point to prove and a legacy to live up to. The point for him was to keep his brother's name alive by any means necessary. Respect was put on Tank's name, due to the fact that he had robbed and killed the plug that afternoon. Before dying in the high-speed chase, Tank had stashed a few pounds of dope and a couple stacks of cash under his bed. Finding that was all it took for Justin to become "J-money." J-money was the new beast on the block. He determined that he was never going to be broke again. Once the money started rolling in, he didn't hesitate to put his boys on with him. All of our lives changed in a few weeks.

The money was coming so fast that we didn't know what to do with it. Once again, we were just living for the moment. The only difference is that we suddenly had money, power, and respect.

Learn from the mistakes of others. You can't live long enough to make them all yourself.

Chapter Three: Mistakes Made and Lessons Learned

We all knew that we would be making money someday. We just had no idea that it would be that soon and that way. J-money was loving every moment. He was making major money and spending it like crazy. He was the only fifteen-year-old pulling up in Infinities and Cadillac trucks. He didn't even have a driver's license. Terrance and I begged him to slow down, but that wasn't an option for him, especially with the kind of money he was bringing in.

While we were constantly in his ear telling him to slow down, there were others who enjoyed the ride and told him the opposite. So he assumed we were jealous of his hustle. J-money started hanging out with the wrong crowd, and he found a new connection. I didn't know anything about the new connection, just that he lived in California.

Suddenly the block was jumping so hard. J-money was getting product shipped every other weekend. And his mother began receiving calls about his not attending school. He was never at home long. So, when he came in the house on this particular day, she stopped him. She asked, "Where have you been?"

He was just standing there, dressed as if it were the first day of school. She was asking questions to get clarification, and J-money replied, "Oatmeal is better than no meal." He then walked out of the house without so much as looking back at the woman who had given him life. She called Terrance and me for answers, but we continued to show our loyalty to our friend. She wouldn't accept the fact that we knew nothing. She pleaded with us. Finally, all we could say was that she should ask around on the streets. We knew our friend was caught up in a lifestyle that could lead to only two conclusions: prison or death.

Our not telling his mother only added to the problem. It left J-money on the streets while costing us her trust. And she was left to stress over her son every day and night with no relief in sight. Fortunately, Terrance and I weren't in too deep. We hoped that if we let go, maybe Justin would do the same. Unfortunately, it was too late for him. Before the street lights came on that next evening, J-money was arrested while meeting with his drug contact from California. He had no idea that the contact had been the police the whole time. His heart sank out of his chest when he was surrounded by all those policemen. With his childlike mind-set, J-money thought this type of thing only happened on television. Not once during his time as a hustler had he sees this as a real possibility.

Just contemplating what my friend was going through gave me a headache that was out of this world. Everybody at school was trying to discuss his situation with us, which made things worse. I was so ready to get out of school before I said something to these people that I might regret. They didn't understand that even though he was my friend, I couldn't give them information, because I didn't know anything myself.

Time doesn't stop for any man. Situations can throw things your way in a split second, good or bad, that can change your life forever. Later that day, I received a phone call from Justin's mom. She was crying and screaming repeatedly, "Eight to fifteen years, Chris!" At that moment, I didn't feel bad hearing the information, because deep down I had known this day would come. I hate that I didn't get to talk to my homie before he went to jail. It was better for him to be locked up and living life rather than dead in a grave, to be seen no more. I hoped and prayed I would see my homie another day.

Terrance and I agreed to never go down that path. With a long life ahead of us, we started thinking about the most important thing in a young boy's life: girls, girls, and more girls. Our hormones were raging, and the girls were developing more and more every day. We couldn't look at a girl without using our imaginary X-ray vision. I know it should be against the law, but you can never get in trouble for your thoughts.

Going into my eighth-grade year with my chest poked out and my nose in the air, I was ready and willing to sex anything that came my way. I thought the easiest way to get sex was to have money. It was either that or play basketball. All the girls wanted a ball player in my day. In their minds, any ball player was, or could be, the next Michael Jordan.

With that being said, basketball tryouts were coming up the following week. Terrance and I were playing one-on-

one every afternoon, waiting for tryouts. I was kicking his butt every time we played. He couldn't do anything against my sick crossover and reverse layups. However, during tryouts the coach thought otherwise. Terrance made the team, and I didn't. *Angry* wasn't the word to describe how I felt. I played a great game at tryouts. I was crossing people every way like Derrick Rose on the court. But the coach had the nerve to tell me I was too flashy. "What? Too flashy? I scored all the points during the game," I said.

Coach replied, "Exactly my point, you scored all the points and forgot about your teammates. There is no *I* in team, Chris."

Disappointed, I began to walk home, mad at the world. Terrance ran up behind me. He said, "Bro, calm down and just try again next year."

"Why should I try again next year?" I snarled. "Why should I take advice from you anyway? I'm a much better player than you. Don't forget it was my idea to try out in the first place. You know I'm better than you, and I should have made the team."

Silence followed that surly statement.

A couple days passed, and we still hadn't communicated. Word had gotten around school that Terrance made the team. I don't know if it was jealousy or if I sensed a dramatic lifestyle change in my best friend. All the girls were in his face constantly, along with some guys who had never given either of us the time of day before. Watching him walk right past me in his letterman's jacket, I entertained plenty of negative thoughts even though I knew it was my fault that we were having problems. At the end of the day, I put my pants on just like him, so apologizing at this time was not an option for me.

It's crazy how one bad disagreement can really make you question yourself about the people you choose to hang out with. Terrance decided to settle down with the most beautiful girl in school, Lisa. She was the captain of the cheerleading squad. They were the perfect match, or so it seemed. On the sideline of every game, she was there cheering him on. The love she seemed to have for him meant more than anything in this world to Terrance. But being a true friend, I could sense that she was a fraud. Real recognizes real, and I was convinced this girl was a snake. Sneaky was her middle name. I know I'm wrong for judging a book by its cover, but my instincts were telling me Lisa was too good to be true.

A friendship

that can end

never really

began!

Chapter Four: Friendships Tested

Once J-Money was incarcerated, I started going back to church. My skating-rink days were over. During church service I was scrolling down my Instagram, and all I saw was Terrance and Lisa. I instantly logged out and signed on to Snapchat. Once again, I saw Terrance and his girl kissing, hugging, and playing love songs in the background of the videos. I was beginning to have enough of them. I had to find some information on Lisa, even if I had to make it up. My best friend was blinded by love.

I hated to come between them, but for her to just come into his life so quickly, I was just shocked. They fell in love so fast, and I had a notion to put an end to it. I felt that Terrance and I would have been back cool by then if it hadn't been for this butter-head tramp distracting my homie.

I began to follow her around school, waiting to capture the moment of her screwing up. My phone had a camera installed in my favorites. You could call me Photographer Chris, because I was locked and loaded at any given moment. Months passed by, and the basketball team was doing great. Terrance was receiving more playtime. He was even scoring a few baskets. At least that was what I was hearing around school. I had to go see that with my own eyes, because the last time I had seen his skills he was getting spanked in the backyard.

I decided to finally catch a game and show my support, which in hindsight might have been a bad idea. Two minutes into the first quarter, Terrance got subbed into the game. Lots of clapping and screaming began when he stepped onto the court, especially from the bleachers where the cheerleaders were stationed. I had no clue they treated him like a star on the court. The referee blew the whistle, ordering them to take the ball out. Posted at the three-point line, the point guard waited for the ball to touch his hands and then passed the ball to Terrance with no hesitation. The whole crowd put three fingers in the air while saying "Threeeee."

Terrance pulled up, with his feet kicked up like Kobe, and from that play on there wasn't anything the defense could do with him. But then the most tragic thing happened: he was on his way up for a layup and stumbled over his own feet, preventing the basket and causing him to fall to the floor. Holding his leg, he writhed in pain. The entire atmosphere changed when he was rolled out on that stretcher. Lisa dropped her pom-poms and followed Terrance and the medical personnel out the door. Even though Terrance had no idea I had attended the game, I was going to go to the hospital to show my support.

Thoughts were going through my head as I walked inside the emergency room: Had Terrance seen me in the stands? Would he be laid out in a hospital bed?

Taking a deep breath as I pulled back the curtains, I saw that his mother and Lisa were the only two there. I stood there like I had never seen them before, until his mother welcomed me like I had never left. She realized that I hadn't been around in a while and began to question him and me. Terrance didn't want to be involved in the conversation, but he couldn't ignore his mother or open up in front of his lady. I was already feeling guilty for no apparent reason. I really couldn't handle the fact that I was somewhere I wasn't wanted. Terrance turned over on his bed, and Lisa looked at me then put her head down. That was my hint to leave, so I gave his mom a hug and went out the door without looking back.

After you're in the hospital for a whole week, people tend to miss you—or at least act like it. Terrance walked into the school on crutches. It seemed as if everybody was waiting for him to arrive. He drew attention like never before. They acted like he had died and come back to life, and he was feeding right into it. As Terrance started feeling better, Lisa started acting like a groupie (given how much she had been doting on him). She was bending over backward for selfish Terrance. The glory and fame was way beyond his comprehension. Seeing her by his side through the shine and struggle made me have second thoughts about her. So when I caught her walking in the hallway alone, I asked her if she would mind having lunch with me after school. She answered yes without hesitation. Let the investigation begin!

When the final bell rang for the day, Lisa scuffled around to find Terrance and got a casual one-arm hug and a peck on the forehead from him. Then she met up with me behind the school to start what could be called our first date. I gave her a real hug, which she hadn't had in a while, and then she began pouring her heart out to me. She talked about Terrance this and Terrance that, and I just smiled and said, "I feel your pain," after every statement she made. As we walked inside Popeye's Chicken, she continued to talk. I stopped her and asked, "Don't you miss how someone acts when you first meet?" I saw the flash in her eyes and the upside-down smile on her face. Even though her tears were dry, I could see them falling down her face. Lisa felt used and neglected like a dirty rag. Looking into her eyes and rubbing her fingers with my thumb, I began to think of her in a very different way.

She had me feeling some type of way. There was a connection between us that we both realized. You can never judge a book by its cover. All you can do is keep turning the page and get deeper into the story. Terrance would not realize he had a good thing until it was gone. I found myself wondering if Terrance would ever get his act together, because I was beginning to like how things were going with Lisa and me. She and I forgot all about eating, because we were caught up in the moment. We decided to exchange numbers, and from that point we walked out of Popeye's Chicken and into each other's lives.

Chapter Five: Betrayal or Blessing

Just the week before, I had been feeling miserable without my guy Terrance. Now I was focused on Lisa. I felt a little jealous about Lisa at first, but then I realized the joke was on Terrance, and he had no idea. Lisa continued to walk behind him, smiling and winking every time she saw me. He continued to walk straight past me like I was invisible. There was no hope in my eyes that he and I would ever be the same. I could only imagine how things would turn out if he found out his girl and I were on the phone every night.

We were texting during classes, sending each other emojis, and every now and then sneaking off after school for a bite to eat. While we both were keeping a secret from Terrance, the entire school was keeping a secret from us. Little did we know, Terrance and Lisa's best friend, Jessica, had been messing around. Good thing Lisa wasn't the type to tell her friends everything. Jessica was also on the cheerleading squad. It is so sad how females can gossip all day about another person's problems, but then they forget to mention an indelicate affair. (Well, I guess you could say men do the same, but in my defense, Terrance and I weren't friends at that moment. Back to the drama.)

Jessica was actually six weeks pregnant with his baby. It's strange how Facebook will tell you everything you need to know. As Lisa read the post to me, I was lost for words, with nothing to say. On the other hand, *she* had plenty of negative words to say. She even threw some comments my way as well—even though I had had no idea any of this was going on. That was the last thing she wanted to hear. Feeling like everyone was against her, pain and betrayal were jumbled up in her heart. Her heart was full of hurt feelings, but the Christian spirit within her wouldn't let her stoop to their level. Killing us with kindness was what she decided to do.

While dealing with all this surprising drama, I received a phone call from a weird number. Having every intention of ignoring it, I became more curious to see who it was. As I picked up the receiver, a familiar voice I couldn't quite recognize was calling my name. "Chris, Chris, Chris!" So I answered and heard, "Bro, what's up?" I knew instantly it was J-Money. Just the man I needed to talk to. I was so glad I had answered the call. It had been two long years since I had heard his voice. We had a lot of catching up to do in the twenty minutes he had to talk. I got straight to the point of my falling out with Terrance. From the beginning to the end, I filled him in on the drama, not even allowing him a chance to speak.

His reply let me know that he was learning a lot in jail. He wasn't J-Money anymore. Justin simply said, "No matter the weather, the world will continue to spin. Once good friends, always good friends until the end. If you guys are clever, you should get it together."

I know he didn't want to hear that we were on bad terms, but his message helped me out. I looked at things totally different from that point on, realizing we had forgotten that we had a homie who couldn't even use the bathroom in private.

Shaking my head, I realized Terrance and I should be ashamed of ourselves. Justin's words of wisdom were locked in my soul. I had to share them with no one else other than my good friend Terrance. I had to man up and try to get things right between us. I understood he might be going through a lot at the moment. During lunch, I saw my guy looking depressed. It was looking as if his fame had gone from one hundred to zero quick. I went up to him as humbly as I could. A grown-man handshake with a pat on the back was all it took for my guy and me to start a revealing conversation.

It seemed that I was talking to a different person. We didn't discuss or share any positive energy or childhood memories. Terrance was talking about how he was going to survive. He was no longer living for himself. Before I could even start telling him about my conversation with Justin, I realized he had started to think like J-Money. He said, "I got to do whatever I got to do."

He was walking in different shoes from mine, but my job as a friend was to tell him that is not the only way. I explained to him that this was the reason Justin was not with us now. We have to learn from the next man's mistakes. When I asked if he was going to throw his basketball career out the window, his only response was, "I have a baby on the way. I need money, and I need it now." I figured Terrance was just having a bad day and he didn't mean any of these dumb comments he was stating. I was just happy to have some form of communication with him again. I didn't want to ruin it by preaching to him like his father. I knew that was the last thing he wanted to hear.

After getting things understood with the homies, I had to get some things understood with Lisa. She agreed to have lunch with me at our favorite fast-food restaurant. She seemed more excited than I was. I was very shocked with the way she hugged me. The way Lisa had wigged out the other day, I had no idea she had that in her. She began to apologize for storming out on me the previous week and admitted that she had let her emotions get the best of her. With my trying to be a forgiving individual, I was happy to see her happy. It brought the excitement out of me. After I attempted to persuade her to never cut me off like that again, she agreed only if I didn't mention anything about "us" to Terrance. With a slow nodding of my head, I agreed to her mischievous statement. Lisa had the strangest smirk on her face, and we hugged to seal the deal—her with a passion to get closer and closer into my life only to ruin it for the better, not having a thought that what goes around comes around, which she could not have cared less about because she was intent on revenge.

Everything in life is temporary. If things are going good, enjoy it because it won't last forever. If everything is going bad, don't worry because it won't last forever.

Chapter Six: The Struggle Died, and a Hustler Was Born

During this time, things in my household weren't a walk in the park. Alexis was getting older, and it was every blue moon that we got to see our mother. The hustle and drive she was showing to keep food on the table was unbelievable. I can count on one hand how many hours of sleep my mother got a day. I wasn't feeling her pain, but the thought of it was killing me. I was old enough to realize she was making money but not old enough to realize where it was going. Bills never stopped coming, and every month a notice came in the mail.

While I was in my room mad about the fact that I wasn't able to get the new Jordan shoes, my mother was sitting in the car praying that it would crank up. But it didn't. The transmission went out on her 1999 Buick. That was the last thing she had expected to happen. Every dollar made a difference in my household. With only one income coming in, the question was whether to pay the bills or to handle the car repair. That was not a hard decision to make. Her checks weren't enough to balance both of these requirements. She had to pay bills instead of getting the car fixed. This would have been the perfect time to have a man around.

Financially, I still was a little boy. I was broke, with no vision for anything. I witnessed the fact that, even though the car was parked in the driveway, my mother still had the drive to move forward and get to work on time each and every day. From that point on, I knew it was no more excuses. There would be no more time to waste, no more thinking that things would just fall out of the sky. The only way I would have things in life would be if I went out to get them.

Of course, that fast money was the first idea in my head. It was very hard to shake it. The dope mentality ran through my veins, that being the only hustle I knew. But with images of my father in my mind, I realized that it would only end in one of two ways: death or time in prison. Thoughts of my father helped me to shake that thought out of my head.

A job was the last thing on my mind, but something had to be done and fast. Application after application, it seemed as if my days were longer and my weeks were shorter, and I still hadn't received a call about a job interview. That is when a Plan B became mandatory. Time had never been so valuable to me. While in the store buying some hot chips and juice, I thought that I wanted to do something different and stay out of trouble. I asked myself what I was good at. The cashier told me my price, and I began to scratch my head and repeat, "Two seventy-two?"

"Dang," I thought, "with only two dollars and seventy-five cents in my pocket, this stuff is starting to get high," and I gave up my last few dollars. A little lightbulb turned on in my head. "Chips and juice! That's it! I can sell chips and juice at school." I couldn't have thought of any idea that would be better. Chips and juice would sell themselves.

All I had to do was keep it on deck. From that moment on, I was on a paper chase. Figuring out that it takes money to make money, I didn't have many dollars to start with. I wondered if maybe one little sin wouldn't hurt to get me on my feet. Asking God for my forgiveness for the wrong I was about to commit, I headed to the local Walmart around the way. That is where I placed multiple bags of chips and a case of juices into the shopping cart, then walked out of the store with no hesitation or regrets at all. When I got home from completing my mission, I began to calculate my "profit." In a week's time, I would be able to make $300. That was $60 a day. "Free bands, free bands," is what I shouted out proudly. Just the thought of making that cash put a wide smirk on my face.

Early Monday morning, waking up with a million-dollar mind-set, I had a variety bag of hot chips with ice-cold juice to drain them down with. This was all high-school kids needed to keep them going. Basically, a profitable provider is what I was. Yes, I was the only guy in the school that had food for sale, and it didn't take long for the word to spread. It was almost as if I was selling crack. The dollars came in, and before I knew it, there wasn't any more product left. The sad part about it all—it wasn't even lunchtime yet. The first day was more than successful. I thought to myself, "I could actually get used to this."

The following day, students were waiting for me. "Dang," I said, "you all must not have eaten this morning."

They must have loved these hot chips, because people were surrounding me as if I was getting jumped into a gang. Reaching to the very bottom of my book bag, I realized once again there wasn't anything in it. Several disappointed students wandered off, with the exception of one person, Terrance.

"What's good?" said Terrance. "I heard you was slanging and had to see that with my own eyes. The eyes never lie, but humans do. Isn't that right, Chris? Ha-ha-ha, hot chips! You slanging hot chips and juice? Maybe I just didn't get a clear understanding."

"Maybe you didn't, my brother, maybe you didn't," I replied.

Then Terrance said, "Tell me if I have a clear understanding about this then, homie. Are you and Lisa dating?"

"Maybe, maybe not," I answered aggressively.

Terrance then stared me up and down. "OK, OK, say no more, homie," he said. "Good luck with your corner-store business. Make sure you watch your surroundings at all times." He let go an evil laugh as he walked off the school campus without looking back.

So I got to thinking hard on how all that hostility came about. And after hiding my juices in the bottom of the refrigerator, away from my thirsty sister, I prepared for another day to make another dollar. While scrolling down Facebook, I discovered some shocking news. Bam, I felt like I got smacked right in the face. Lisa had announced we were a couple—right there on Facebook. Things were starting to add up now, and I understood Terrance's hostility.

Chapter Seven: Exposure

I dialed Lisa's number instantly. I wanted to ask her why I wasn't informed of the surprise. We had been low-key all that time, so for her to go behind my back and inform the world surprised me. The sad part is that the information was not true. Like any woman would, she reversed that accusation on me as quickly as possible. I really think she had already been prepared for my reaction.

"Really, Chris?" Lisa said. "I'm not worth a title? How long where you planning to keep us a secret? All these walks home and lunch dates didn't mean a thing, huh?"

In total shock, I replied, "What does any of that have to do with your saying we are in a relationship in a very public way? You got me all over Facebook for the world to see." It was the reason Terrance came at me like he did.

Apparently, I didn't whisper Terrance's name softly enough. "Terrance, Terrance?" screamed Lisa. "So this is why you're asking me these questions? You're worried about what *Terrance* thinks? And to think that he doesn't even care about you at all. He always spoke down on your name, especially when Justin left."

The way things were going, it wasn't hard to believe what she was saying. A lot of thoughts ran through my mind. But I had to take into consideration that this was the same girl who buried my friendship with Terrance in the mud. It was not long before I complied, so I invited Lisa over. I got tired of arguing. After sex and a good night's sleep, my nose was wide open. The next day, I agreed to the relationship scheme.

With my name in everybody's mouth, it seemed like I had the juice now. Money was still the motto, and fame would follow behind it. I was used to watching everybody else in the spotlight. I grinded hard to complete my goal, which was to get my mother's car fixed. She was so happy to see me step up to the plate, and she had no idea that the blessing had her name on it. I was excited to impress my mother, but I was more eager to entertain the public. I attracted a very large crowd. Everybody wanted to be my friend and follow in my footsteps. I was enjoying being the center of attention.

As a young entrepreneur, I was getting money, and I wasn't afraid to show the world. On Facebook I was a star, bankrolls on every picture, even though I had a lot of one-dollar bills underneath. The attention was very appealing and thrilling for me. The need for more money was thumping like a heartbeat. It was a must that I find a way to generate more money at a faster rate. Building a team with a couple of strangers wasn't a bad idea. I hired some guys who were friends with Lisa. She told me they were the right guys for the job. I believed her without a doubt, with no questions asked. I started Johnny, Tavaris, and Robert off with sixty dollars' worth of product each. I expected to collect $180 at the end of the day. "Let's see what these guys are about," I thought.

Waiting patiently for that cash to touch the palms of my hands, I was walking around school without a bag on my shoulder, wondering if these guys were making any progress. As I looked up, the guys were coming around the corner, looking like a mob. The bell had just rung for lunch, and they all approached me with empty bags. I was looking confused until I saw them reaching into their pockets. A huge smile appeared on my face as they begun to pull money out. "I might be on the verge of building an empire, I thought to myself." I counted it up—things had gone beyond well the first day.

Lisa and I celebrated by having a full-course meal at a restaurant whose name we couldn't pronounce. I was so anxious to make more money. I started sharing all of my business ideas with Lisa. She just sat there without saying a word. Her deep dimples showed a perky smile on her face, and her ears were wide open, programming every word I said into her brain. Instead of having the same vision as I had, Lisa had an empire of her own that she was focusing on.

On the other hand, things weren't looking so pretty for Terrance. His baby's arrival was getting closer and closer all the time. He wasn't making enough money, and he didn't see a future in furthering his high-school career. And money wasn't his only problem. Baby-mama drama came along with it. She craved for this and that, so every dollar he did make was already spent. He did whatever to keep Jessica satisfied, because what he didn't provide, child support would. The world was crumbling down upon his shoulders. Having nobody to run to or talk to had him mad at the world. And Justin's back was against the wall. The streets were his support system, but nothing but negativity had come out of that. Even though I wasn't selling dope, I was making a lot of money. All a broke person had to do was scroll down Facebook to see that I had become a target.

While browsing the Internet, Terrance looked over my pictures with an evil laugh. He devised a plan. Seeing me hugged up with his old girl cemented his hatred for me. In an instant, he decided that getting back in Lisa's good graces would push her away from me. Not stopping to ask God for guidance, for leading in the right direction, he settled and was looking forward to taking the easy way out, to only make a name and collect temporary change. Forgetting about all the good times and reflecting on the bad, Terrance was willing to put his friend's life in danger over money, girls, and good times.

Chapter Eight: More Money, More Problems

Weeks went on by, and business was still booming for me. Unexpected blessings were falling out the sky. I treated myself by purchasing a drop-top Mustang. It was pearl white with a peanut-butter top, and it had a sandy-brown interior with some brand-new seventeen-inch factory wheels. The town wasn't ready for that, and to be honest, I wasn't either. I had an image to maintain, and what better way than being the only eleventh grader with a grown-man whip? I was really giving the city something to talk about now.

When I slid through the student parking lot for the first time in my new whip, all the students' necks broke as the top slowly began to rise up. Everyone surrounded the vehicle while taking pictures and videos with their phones. Star status once again struck like lightning. Lisa came out of the crowd, wondering what was going on. Shocked to see me gradually stepping out of a vehicle that looked rented—and not looking excited or happy for me at all— she wanted to know the truth.

My smile turned upside-down as Lisa pulled me by my arm away from the car. "Um, what is this?" she yelled.

I stammered back, "What is what? This is my new whip!"

My smile disappeared as Lisa showed no signs of being happy for me. The fussing and cursing she was doing went in one ear and out the other. Lisa noticed my ignoring her and took that moment to remind me that none of this would have been possible without her.

Upset by her response, I replied, "Lisa, I will eat with or without you!" Holding back my tongue probably would've been best in this situation. The way things were stirring up, nobody was going to be in my corner anymore.

Lisa walked away from me, and Terrance decided at that moment to get in where he fit in. Only saying hi to Lisa, he made her feel some type of way. He could see the spark in her eyes as if she had been waiting on that moment. She didn't realize what she was getting into. By just saying a few words and mentioning a couple of memories, Terrance got Lisa to giggling, and that boosted his confidence through the roof. He was about to be on her like flies on a stink pile. The way I had been avoiding her, she was dying for attention. Lisa figured Terrance was the perfect person to get it from.

While everyone was pretty much plotting, trying to make my life miserable, I was plotting how to keep money coming in throughout the summer. Writing my ideas down helped a lot. Out of the several possible things I was capable of doing, party promoting was the most interesting of them all. With the city support and social media, advertising was going to be easy. I just needed more capital to put my thoughts in motion. Even if I had to slang more bags of candy, chips, and juice, it would be worth it. With only a couple months left of my junior year in high school, I needed to get that money in a timely manner. As I said before, time waits for no man, so if I wanted it, I had to go out and get it.

Chapter Nine: New Hustle, Same Problems

It was grind time, and everyone was forming a mentality to go get it. Summer time was a few days away, and senior year was around the corner. It was getting down to the wire, and a lot of soon-to-be grown-ups were still confused. On the other hand, the teenagers that were starving thought of a plan. Why not just take from a walking bankroll? That walking bankroll was me, of course. My own friend was scheming on me. Positioning Lisa back in his life would make it much easier. But when and how would he know to educate her on the good news? What if she was not on the same page?

Luckily, when they decided to meet up, she started off complaining to Terrance about her problems with me. He figured that his plan may be easier than he thought.

Terrance sat back and just let her go on and on. Lisa was talking about how she did this and how she did that. She finished off by wishing for a way to take away my glory. In reality, all she wanted was for me to notice her.

With that being said, Terrance was going to put her thoughts in action by throwing ideas in her ear and trying to expand her mind even more. It made me seem very negative from her point of view. Lisa was ready to fall back into Terrance's arms, forgetting that she would be playing stepmom. Nowhere in the discussions did he mention the baby. He was really surprised at the fact that she didn't bring it up. Terrance was happy and trying to accomplish his goal as soon as possible.

There was no doubt that I was handling business. Only two weeks were left before the summer break. Hustling and promoting at the same time is what I was doing. I came up with an idea to throw an "NBA" party. NBA was short for

"Nothing but A——," and this was expected to be a major event. The whole school was talking about the party. It was really something to look forward to. Even though it was a couple of months away, the early promotion would keep everyone's schedule clear.

Lisa was kind of having the best of both worlds, or maybe she was stuck between a rock and a hard place. Unfortunately, she put herself in this situation. Only wanting to be in the limelight, she ended up being the butt of a joke. It was crazy that she still wasn't smart enough to realize that.

Experience is the best teacher. Instead of her heart getting broken in half, I guess she needed it broken into pieces, because things just weren't clicking. Lisa needed help before things got out of hand. The middle is where she would be between two ex–best friends. Things can become very serious in the blink of an eye. Only time would tell.

In the meantime, Justin reached out to both Terrance and me. Speaking to Justin, Terrance said that I had been on some real fake stuff since I was making some money. Justin wanted to reminisce about the old days when things were good, but Terrance said that things were not good in the streets anymore. "You must be dreaming, homie," said Terrance. "Things are going downhill in these streets."

From my point of view, Terrance should have just been speaking for himself, because things were going good for me. With my not being able to defend myself, Terrance was throwing me under the bus and feeding Justin plenty of false information regarding their friendship. Terrance took bits of the truth and turned things around. I changed my phone number, and Justin couldn't get in touch with me, so the truth would remain untold. Until Justin got his feet on the ground, his brain would continue to be stained with a lie.

Truthfully, Terrance or I wouldn't have made it in Justin's shoes. I was too arrogant, and Terrance was an unforgiving individual. These personalities can't adapt in a jail cell. Both of us were blinded by the fact that we got a chance to see the light of day every morning and woke up with another chance to better ourselves. While Justin was praying every day for another opportunity, and praying that his friends would get it together and try to better themselves, Terrance and I were pretty much taking life for granted. We were missing the big picture of how things used to be, when we were coming up. Not learning from Justin's mistakes, Terrance and I let pride stand in the way of our friendship. I guess it's all part of becoming men.

Pride wasn't the only thing standing in the way of our friendship. Lisa still was the white cream between two Oreo cookies. She was about to walk in on a reminder that Justin still had a baby on the way. Focusing on revenge against me, she forgot all about Terrance and Jessica until she overheard a group of ladies discussing it in the hair shop. It caught her by surprise and changed her whole thought process immediately. Instead of ruining my life and trying to trust Terrance, in her eyes both of us could go jump in a lake.

I had no idea any of this negativity was coming my way. Lisa was against me, which turned my workers away as well. It really didn't matter, because the summer was beginning. Terrance hated my guts, and he wanted to be in my position. Instead, his life was still going downhill. A thundercloud was following him every step of the way. With back-to-back visits with Jessica and going to and from the doctor, Terrance was due to become the father of a baby girl any day.

That was really freaking Terrance out. He had yet to make a major move to get back on his feet. It was time for him to stop beating around the bush with Lisa and complete his plot against me. Hanging out with Lisa again really did a number on his head. He and Lisa had memories, but he and Jessica were making history. Responsibility Road was around the corner from Manhood Lane. It was only a matter of time before he would get the job done.

Terrance got his hands on one of my fliers for the party. He decided this would be the perfect day to stretch me. He called Lisa to have a discussion about the robbery. She figured it would be a good idea, knowing that I would have a lot of cash on me. I was known to show off at a party. The closest people to me were watching me like a hawk. Instead of getting in on their own business, they focused on taking the other king's throne.

You would think Terrance would have second thoughts about doing this to his friend. But he didn't care at all—he needed cash fast. Lisa just really wanted to be a part of something. Thinking this was the perfect way to seek revenge, she didn't want anybody to get hurt. She didn't know whose side to really be on. She was really mad at both of us, but she got stuck in Terrance's mess. There would be no turning around from this point on.

Chapter Ten: Finding Your Purpose

Being afraid to take a chance in life will hold you back. Fear is the most destructive disease for humans. There is no benefit or plus to plotting on someone. You don't have to be Einstein in order to put a dollar in your pocket. Life is about finding your purpose, and that will make you a better person. All I did was travel my own road and leave a trail. If I did it, they could too. If they had put the same effort into working on themselves as they did in focusing on me, maybe they would be going into their senior year with a plan.

One of the craziest things about this generation is that they are young minded. They still have time to figure out who they want to become. Sadly, instead of using me as a motivational guide, they chose to hate. But it truly takes more energy to hate someone than it does to love him.

Commitment in your life means taking action. I decided to have my party on July 4. Everybody from all over was looking forward to this day. It had been a while since the community had had a major event to look forward to. I was making a difference within my generation. I had more power than I realized. And I was coming from being a young man that never had anything. That was my excuse, and it was my reason to show off. Everybody didn't see eye to eye or know where I came from. All they could do was watch me slide through the city and take action.

My name was getting out there because I was promoting each and every day. Networking and staying active in church were making this party a success. People

from my church were volunteering to help, and even

schoolteachers wanted to help. My teachers remembered

times I saved their stomachs with bags of chips and a

refreshing beverage—keeping in mind that everything in

life is temporary. If it's going good, enjoy it, because it

might not last forever.

One week away from the party of the year, gifted as I

am, I had everything organized. I was more than prepared

for this life-changing event that was about to take place. I

figured I owed all my thanks to God in heaven. I expressed

that by taking my mother and sister out to lunch.

Unfortunately, they were really the only two who stayed

the same through this journey. While sitting in Zaxby's

with two young ladies that I loved dearly, I decided to

express my feelings. I started by letting them know that I

loved them. Words could not express what my life would be without them.

"You ladies have been down with me through the shine and the struggle," I said. "Little sister, girl, you know I love you. You will never be too old for me to kiss and hug you. Just make sure when you get a boyfriend, he must be a hustler. Mom, words can't even explain the pain that you have been through. I know it's etched in your mind. Trust me; I'm going to make a change."

As a family, it's a must that we express our feelings toward one another. One's life is a book that is already written, and we as humans have no idea when our last day is going to come. So make the best of it while you can.

Unfortunately, people wake up feeling a different type of way each and every day. Days rolled by, and it was the official day for my huge party. I woke up neither happy nor sad. A strange tingle flowed through my body. The feeling kind of placed me in a box, and I wondered how the night might turn out. I then went downstairs and saw a big smile on my mother's face. That made all the negative thoughts disappear. She said, "Chris, I'm proud to call you my son. You really deserve this. You went down your own path and separated yourself. That's the main important part in becoming a man. A lot of people look up to you, including me—yes I said it, including me. You are a gifted young man with a plan." She then grabbed me by the hand and said, "Now, turn up tonight!"

After those inspirational words spoken to me from my mother, I felt like, why not go to the mall and find a fresh outfit for the night? In the midst of my walking through different stores, almost everybody in there approached me like I was a celebrity. Ladies yelled, "Hey, Chris, see you tonight. I'm not wearing any panties tonight!" Oooweee, the recognition was real in the field. Girls were coming from left and right to be part of this party. It really made me

forget all about Lisa. Normally, Lisa would have at least

texted or called, complaining about something. I noticed I

hadn't talked to her in a couple of days, but I didn't care at

the moment because there were plenty of fish in the sea.

Instead, Lisa was too busy putting together my surprise

after party. Terrance and Lisa were going to be my special

guests. The plan was to let me enjoy my party but to catch

me later by my car. They figured I would have no idea who

did it with all the commotion going on outside the event. I

might just have extra cash in the car also, or so they

thought. If everyone didn't know my car, that would have

been on their list too. Instead, Terrance and Lisa had

planned a quick masked robbery. They knew I didn't have

a gun. I was too much of a Goody-Two-shoes to be on that

level. So Lisa convinced Terrance not to use a real gun—or

so she thought. Terrance was highly upset about that

decision. From being on the streets, he abided by the street rules. It's better to be caught with than without his "strap." Things can backfire at any given moment, and he was willing to throw that fire back if necessary. He couldn't afford to be caught slipping. He had a baby due sooner than he could imagine.

Chapter Eleven: Stressing for a Blessing

The day of the party, Terrance got an unexpected phone call. Jessica called him from a hospital phone, explaining in a panicked tone that her water had broken. She said that she had been calling him for several hours. She had been rushed to the hospital. This was a very unusual experience for her. She was scared out of her mind and needed a support system by her side. In the middle of sealing the deal with Lisa, he had to rush to the emergency room to be

Jessica's support system. "A few hours before the party and this pop up," said Terrance. Having arrived at the hospital with her hair all over the place and soaking wet from sweat, Jessica was hot in a cold building and nervous in a protective environment. She was excited to see Terrance's face in the place.

The line was wrapped around the building at the party spot. People were dancing to the music playing inside. Given a ratio of five girls to one guy, I was enjoying the view. Opening the doors to my event felt like opening the gates of heaven. Seeing all these people walk through the door instantly gave me butterflies in my stomach. I was just smiling to think of how much I would profit, while thanking the good Lord for the opportunity. It was amazing how people were continuously walking through the doors from all over the city.

Meanwhile, at the emergency room, it was the total opposite. Only one person was walking back and forth, and that person was Terrance. After asking himself common-sense questions, he still refused to do the right thing, which would have been giving up his revenge plan and not crossing his friend. Lisa being his eyes at the event was making it harder for Terrance to throw in the towel. Lisa was texting him, giving him every detail of what was going on. It was eating Terrance alive to hear that the party was turning out to be successful. He had to get there before it got too late.

Terrance let a couple minutes' pass by to make sure his next move was his best move. The hospital wasn't giving any feedback regarding the arrival time for the baby. That gave Terrance the opening he needed to dismiss himself for a quick second. He had to catch me at the right moment, because one false move or one wasted minute might just throw off the whole plan. Terrance texted Lisa when he arrived in the parking lot. He saw my vehicle and decided to park on the opposite side, even though he was in somebody else's car. Making sure nobody spotted him was his major focus in this situation. He needed this mission to be quick and easy so he could get back to the hospital.

When he finally found a good parking spot, everybody from inside the building began to come out. Lisa kind of stalled and hung around to keep an eye on me. Mind you, she did not want to be seen either. Keeping her distance from me, she watched as hundreds of people scattered all over the place. She did a great job of stalking me. This was an easy assignment because she did it all the time at school. But one glimpse at her phone to see if Justin had texted or called caused her to lose me in the crowd. She got frustrated on account of losing me, so she called Terrance to find out his location and walked over to meet him.

Lisa wasn't excited to approach Terrance with the bad news, but it was a must that she gets to him before I pulled off. "Where he at?" Terrance said as Lisa opened the door to the vehicle.

With a sad look, she replied, "I lost him. In the blink of an eye he was gone." In that instant, Terrance cranked up the car and headed toward my car. My vehicle was already in motion. "See what you did!" Terrance parked the car and yelled at Lisa. An argument between the two ensued. That's when Lisa decided to have no part of the plan anymore. She removed herself from the passenger seat and began to walk back toward the event. Terrance screamed, "So I will do it by myself! I'm not going to let you interfere with my comeuppance."

He continued to follow my vehicle, waiting on a sudden stop to gain the perfect opportunity. Lisa was just as angry as Terrance, but he didn't want to hear her excuse for failing the mission.

In the back of her mind, she felt bad about walking off on him. Lisa regretted the situation even more when she got closer to the event. I was standing in front of the building soaking up the props from the amazing party I had just had. Seeing me made her heart skip a beat. She wondered, "If Chris is right here, then who was driving his car?" Lisa instantly called Terrance to tell him what was going on, but he ignored her calls repeatedly. She really didn't know what to do from that point, since informing me was not an option. The only choice she had was to let nature take its course. And nature was planning for things to get real ugly.

After being in traffic for thirty minutes, Terrance got really impatient following my vehicle around the city. His phone rang again, but this time it wasn't Lisa. It was a call from Jessica—she wanted to know where he was. Her blood pressure was high, what with stressing about the baby and not having her backbone around. He told her that he would be there shortly. Terrance knew now was the time to speed the process up. It was around two in the morning, so the traffic was real dead. Terrance decided that at the next stoplight he would jump out and put the chrome to the driver of the vehicle, who he thought to be me.

So with no second thought, he did just that. He ran up to the driver's side, opened the door, and said, "Give me all your money!" A loud scream from a woman was all he heard. Then in a stuttering tone a voice said, "Te-Te-Te-Terrance?" At that moment, Terrance put the gun down instantly and ran back to the car.

As he zoomed off as fast as he could, he couldn't believe he had just pulled a gun on my mother. The Lord knows how much trouble he had just gotten himself into. There was no way he could get himself out of this. He instantly began to ask God for forgiveness. But he was stuck between a rock and a hard place. He was way past a nervous feeling, more like devastated. He had nowhere to run or hide. If he went home, they would find him. Going to the hospital would be like walking into the police station. A handful of options, with a hundred ways to get caught, was all he had. His life was about to be over, especially when the police came after him.

The secret of living an excellent life is thinking excellent thoughts. It's about programming our minds with information that will set us free.

Chapter Twelve: Life of Excellence

My options had expanded. Except for the niggling problem of which girl, I should be with, life was treating me well because I had chosen to keep God first. I wasn't stressing about anything—not money, respect, or women. I had everything an upcoming twelfth grader should have and more. That's the main reason people around me when I didn't have anything wanted to take from me while I had everything. When you are on the outside looking in, you will always paint a perfect picture of somebody else's life (unless of course you are one of those people walking around with a mean mug from sunup until sundown). But people are hard to read, and your attitude dictates a good day.

Now Terrance would have to be on the run for the rest of his life. He would never have a good day with his involvement on his conscience. It hadn't even been an hour since the incident with my mother, and he was already going insane in the brain. Terrance started to think that it would have benefited him more if he had killed her. Since he missed that opportunity, he decided to kill himself instead.

Terrance drove to the high-school parking lot after the attempted robbery, screaming and crying, with the pistol pointed to his temple. At that moment, he let Satan take control of his life, and he pulled the trigger. Terrance had figured that would solve all his problems, that he would no longer have to deal with anything. He was absolutely wrong about that. His soul was no longer under his command. It would just burn in hell for eternity. That was the worst decision he ever made. That's the worst decision anybody could ever make.

Jessica steadily called Terrance's phone. She was happy that the pain was over and could now see the sparkle in her baby girl's eyes. Upset at the fact that Terrance missed everything, her mother took it upon herself to go find him using the app on her iPhone 6. She had a mouthful to tell him once she saw him, especially since he had been gone all night in her car.

Once she finally found him, the view wasn't what she expected at all. Seeing blood all over her gray leather seats made tears fall like raindrops from her eyes. The Lord knows her heart wasn't ready to handle this situation. After calling the ambulance, she knew Jessica should be the next voice to hear about the tragedy. But how could she tell her daughter that her baby's father was dead on the same day of her granddaughter's birth? The person who had to deliver the bad news was not who she wanted it to be.

Unfortunately, when the ambulance pulled up, so did the local news station. From that point on, the world knew about the teenager found dead in the school parking lot, resulting in a young teenage mother having to raise a daughter in this world alone.

Happiness is a temporary feeling that can be ruined at any given moment. Instead of living a happy life, try living a joyful one. No matter what comes your way, nothing and no one can steal your joy unless you allow them to.

Jessica cried every single night until the official date of the funeral. When she saw Terrance's body tucked in that casket, not one tear came to her eyes. As she looked into her child's face, she was thankful enough to have a part of him with her forever. Having a child is a blessing that teaches a big lesson. So her confession was that there was no need for stressing (even though she still didn't know the actual story).

It's sad how a tragedy brings everybody back together. Lisa and Jessica hadn't been face-to-face in a long time. I even decided to put my pride to the side and walked up to both ladies, requesting a group hug. We came to the conclusion that life is too short. We had to be sure to take advantage of this moment and love one another.

I witnessed that one can be here one day and gone the next. One might even do time in a jail cell, but eventually it will be heaven or hell. The road you take will lead you exactly where you want to be. To make a difference, it's a must that you make a decision. We as kids don't ask to come into this world. Someone else makes the decision to lay down and create a family tree. Justin decided to follow in his brother Tank's footsteps. Terrance made a decision to drop out of school and give up on life. Me, I decided to separate myself by creating my own path through wise decisions.

From my mother's standpoint, she made the decision to never bring up the incident with Terrance. She had never had the idea to call the police on Terrance. She had just asked God to watch over his soul. Terrance's fears got the best of him, forcing him to commit suicide. My mother is the only one who will live to know the truth about Terrance. Meanwhile, everyone continues to remain good friends and continue their journey in the circle of life.

Let us honor the Gospel truth: "For I delivered to you as of first importance what I also received, that Christ died for our sins according to the Scriptures, and that He was buried, and that He was raised on the third day according to the Scriptures, and that He appeared to Cephas, then to the twelve" (1 Cor. 15:3–5 New American Standard Bible). By repenting of our sins and receiving Jesus as our Lord and savior, we can be saved by grace and through faith (Eph. 2:8–9, Rom. 10:9). We should all remember to be thankful for every breath we take and every move in the making.

Don't take any wooden nickels. Put some money aside for

a rainy day, because any given day there might be no food

on your plate. Give grace, just in case someone needs it,

and build a life of excellence.

#SocialShawn

44358291R00055

Made in the USA
San Bernardino, CA
13 January 2017